Long down the road

when our hearts break

we'll finally know

the keeper of faith

THE FAITH KEEPER
Copyright © 2016 by Cindy Palin

All rights reserved. Neither this publication nor any part of this publication may be reproduced or transmitted in any form or by any means, electronic or mechanical, including photocopying, recording or any information storage and retrieval system, without permission in writing from the author.

Unless otherwise indicated, all scripture quotations taken from the Holy Bible, NEW INTERNATIONAL VERSION®. Copyright © 1973, 1978, 1984, 2011 by Biblica, Inc. All rights reserved worldwide. Used by permission. NEW INTERNATIONAL VERSION® and NIV® are registered trademarks of Biblica, Inc. Use of either trademark for the offering of goods or services requires the prior written consent of Biblica US, Inc. Scripture quotations marked (ESV) are taken from The Holy Bible, English Standard Version® (ESV®), copyright © 2001 by Crossway, a publishing ministry of Good News Publishers. Used by permission. All rights reserved. Scripture quotations marked (MSG) are taken from The Message. Copyright © by Eugene H. Peterson 1993, 1994, 1995, 1996, 2000, 2001, 2002. Used by permission of NavPress Publishing Group.

ISBN: 978-1-4866-1160-7 Printed in Canada

Word Alive Press
131 Cordite Road, Winnipeg, MB R3W 1S1
www.wordalivepress.ca

Library and Archives Canada Cataloguing in Publication

Palin, Cindy, 1963-, author
    The faith keeper : long down the road when our hearts break / Cindy Palin.

Issued in print and electronic formats.
ISBN 978-1-4866-1160-7 (paperback).--ISBN 978-1-4866-1161-4 (pdf).--
ISBN 978-1-4866-1162-1 (html).--ISBN 978-1-4866-1163-8 (epub)

    1. Palin, Cindy, 1963-. 2. Women singers--Alberta--Olds--Biography.
3. Women composers--Alberta--Olds--Biography. 4. Women authors--Biography. 5. Faith. I. Title.

ML420.P164A3 2015   782.0092   C2015-907035-X
                                             C2015-907036-8

"Long down the road when our hearts break
we'll finally know the keeper of faith."
—Cindy Palin

Enter through the narrow gate. For wide is the gate and broad is the road that leads to destruction, and many enter through it. But small is the gate and narrow the road that leads to life, and only a few find it.

—Matthew 7:13–14

To my husband:
Thank you for loving me for who I am
and always encouraging me to step out in faith.

To my children:
Rejoice in the life God has given you.
Remember the promise you made,
and be faithful. Finish the race.

Contents

	Last Resort	ix
	Introduction	xi
	Prologue	xiii
1.	The Stirring	1
2.	The Early Middle Years	5
3.	Greener Grass	9
4.	The Rescue Prayer	13
5.	Angry Laments	17
6.	The Seed of Hope	23
7.	Pity Party	29
8.	Seasons	45
9.	An Angel Moves In	55
10.	Life is Short	67
	Epilogue	73
	Resources	75
	About the Author	77

Last Resort

I've been dwellin' on the past, know that I'm forgiven,
but I've got somethin' I want to say to You.
I once chose the wider path, sold my innocence and
Left You nothin' but a broken fool.

In front of the world I made You look like
You were my last resort
In front of the world I made You look like second choice
In front of the world I want to make it clearer than before
You should have been first, You are my everything and more.

So I mourn for those who make my similar mistakes
And marvel at the ones who can choose the truth.
Won't be wastin' words; I'm makin' up for lost time.
Want to spend the rest of my days with You!

"Last Resort" ©2005/Cindy Palin

Introduction

When I first felt the stirring to write, I wasn't sure where to begin. At first my quest for love as a young adolescent spilled out onto the page, stopping short as I prayed beside a bed in a college dorm. I then considered writing in detail about the path of searching itself, which every man, woman, and child must travel at some time during our short stay here on Earth. As I analyzed the vignettes of yesteryear, a powerful revelation moved to the forefront. *What puzzles me more?* I wondered. *My search for love, or my inability to be faithful once love has found me?*

Love finds us and calls us towards eternity, but when the going gets tough, we want to quit. The journey of faith stops in the middle for so many. Such is the condition of the fickle human heart.

Much of my story shared here is from the middle years when all the colours of the world tried to paint love grey. The honeymoon stage of faith had faded, and my beliefs were challenged by the harsh realities around me. A tsunami in Asia and a letter from Africa were instrumental in stirring my spirit. A rescue prayer followed and set in motion several unexpected, life altering events, which alerted me to the late hour in which I live.

I was awakened from a seductive spell to "surrender" to love once more.

I almost settled for a life of embedded theologies (doing what everyone else does, just because), and almost bought into a culture that promotes position and things, relegating God to second place, or less. I nearly missed out on "[living] *a life worthy of the calling* ... [I] *received*" (Ephesians 4:1). I'd all but decided Jesus wasn't enough, only to find that He's my "everything."

Prologue

"The Road" seems to be a very strong, recurring metaphor in my life, and certainly appears in several of the song prayers I've written over the past thirty years. In some ways the songs are the typical scribblings of an artist trying to make sense of the world, but after going through a study called *Experiencing God*, by Henry T. Blackaby, and completing a course called B.L.A.S.T. (Building Leaders, Authors, Speakers, and Teachers) under the leadership of bestselling author Shannon Ethridge, I discovered something beautiful.

Both authors suggest a powerful exercise in which one goes back in time and notes significant markers on life's road where it was evident God was at work. To my surprise, I found hundreds of road signs in the form of scrawled out verses—some packed away in dusty boxes, others piled high atop my piano, and a select few even recorded. Many of the messages contained a similar thread. My waiting at the piano to put thoughts to paper was actually my spirit postured in prayer, waiting for God to speak. By tracing the lyrics, I could see how His truth had directed my life all along the way. As I read the lyrics, I saw my Faith Keeper pursuing me. I saw people's faces, and how He'd inspired me to write song prayers for them. I saw the people God had prompted to pray on my behalf.

One such person was my grandmother. She was a God-fearing woman, who by God's prompting began praying for me while I was yet in the womb. I am certain of it. I'm also sure she prayed for all of her grandchildren with equal fervour.

My grandmother made many trips down the country road between her house and mine to minister peace to my fearful heart with the words of Psalm 91. I can still hear her voice speaking His words of refuge, rescue, and faithfulness over me.

Our connection was unique. She would sometimes call me in the mornings before school to explain how she'd been awakened during the night to pray for me. On one such occasion, her sleep was disturbed by severe knee pain, and she took it as a sign from God to pray for me. Sure enough, I had injured my knee and was having trouble sleeping.

Her insight did not alarm me. As a child of six on our backyard swing-set, I became aware of God in a very real way. I was pumping my little legs back and forth to get higher in the sky, while singing at the top of my lungs. As my makeshift melody and limited vocabulary filled the early morning air, I noticed the sun crawling over our farmhouse roof and knew God was with me. As the wind graced my brow, I heard Him speak to my spirit—though not audibly—and my child-like faith was born. Our hearts were connected forever with an invisible thread of melodic praise and prayer.

I knew Grandma and I believed in a God who was alive and active in our lives. I knew she and I had a direct line of communication with Him through prayer and song. She too was a musician and composer. I also knew God had connected us in a special way for a reason.

At fifteen years of age I became disillusioned with Christianity due to an inappropriate and damaging sexual advance from a pastor. I told no one about it, and I left the church. There were other deep-seated, generational factors that contributed to my confusion, but the betrayal of a spiritual mentor poisoned my faith. To punish God, I decided to shut His voice out and do my own thing. Deep down I knew that I couldn't blame God for the failings of others, but I shut Him out as best as I could anyway.

After graduating from high school, I took a job at a bank in the city and also began performing with a group called "The Young Canadians." Often I would come home on weekends to visit my boyfriend and family. One weekend a phone call came from Grandma Marie. She'd had a horrible nightmare that I'd been killed in a car accident.

"There was so much blood," she said in a sobering tone. "Will you come in and pray with me?"

Grandma didn't know that my prayer life had fallen silent, but because I respected her and knew that God was still very much alive, I went to her house to pray.

One week later, on Thanksgiving Day, my grandmother's nightmare began to unfold. Little did I know that her obedience in acting on the dream as a warning from God—and my responding to her in respect—would alter the outcome. Ultimately it was God's infinite mercy that intervened. I may have shut my Faith Keeper out, but He is always faithful.

My boyfriend was driving me back into the city and asked if I would roll him a joint. Something inside of me snapped, and I challenged him on his endless dependency on alcohol and drugs. While I heard my indignant words hurl out of my mouth, I knew I had my own crutches and devices. Without thinking, he let go of the wheel to dig into his pocket for supplies. Suddenly I looked up and saw the grass engulfing the windshield. I had just enough time to cry out "Jesus!"

Everything went black as I felt myself fall to the right and into what felt like a warm blanket. Seconds later, I was standing on the left side of the highway, two lanes over, watching the car turn end over end, playing marbles with my boyfriend still inside.

I learned later through the police investigation that I must have been thrown through the windshield before the roof of the car melded to the floorboards. That would explain the shredding of my clothing, still hanging off my body in strips. But there was no blood. I should have been found in the hay field, to the right of where the car initially hit the approach. I should have been dead.

I didn't need to read the report to tell me what I already knew. God had spared my life, as well as my boyfriend's. Jesus had heard my cry and reached down from Heaven. "*Surely the arm of the Lord is not too short to save, nor his ear to dull to hear*" (Isaiah 59:1).

Shamefully, even after such a miraculous intervention, it still took me a couple of years into college before I surrendered completely to His plan for my life.

Love had found me long ago. Love had heard my cry again, so one would think the standard to be sealed. After Christ's endless acts of mercy, should my faith not only grow and strengthen and trump my human condition? But oh the pull of the great divide that lulls us to sleep and rallies our pride!

Chapter One
The Stirring

Dark Eyes

Dark eyes, your wings have been severed;
The life you once treasured now lives only in your mind.
And I cry, 'cause your memories can't hold you,
But believe what they told you,
You're still a very special child.

Dark eyes, your heart has been hollowed;
The evil has swallowed all that you have known,
And my nights are spent praying for rainbows,
For blankets with no holes and someone to call your own.

And I'll find a way to love you, find a way to say
Everything they'd tell you if they hadn't gone away.
And then I'll try
To sing and send to you this lullaby.

Though an ocean divides us, the spirit inside us
Cries for love, cries for love.

> And I'll find a way to love you, find a way to say
> Everything they'd tell you if they hadn't gone away.
> And then I'll try,
> To sing and send to you this lullaby
>
> "Dark Eyes" ©2004/Cindy Palin

My "wake up call" crashed upon the shores of my divided heart in the aftermath of the ocean's assault on Southern Asia in December of 2004. Somehow simple things like enjoying breakfast, or soaking in the sunshine, seemed criminal. During the day, haunting media images shared my shadow. Broadcast banners streamed through my sleep. I was convinced half the world's population lay dead, and the other half were drowning in sadness with me. Like any colossal tragedy, I wondered why so many people had to perish.

"P-e-r i-s-h," I sounded the word out loud.

Ironically it had a soft lyrical flow. Then I remembered where I had first truly noticed the word: *"The Lord is not slow in keeping his promise, as some understand slowness. Instead he is patient with you, not wanting anyone to perish, but everyone to come to repentance"* (2 Peter 3:9).

I knew God's patience to be true in my own life. My grandmother's nightmare and subsequent prayer had served as a warning for me in my youth, and God spared me. But why? Why hadn't God warned the people of Southern Asia? The God I believed in ... the God I talked to ... was capable of posting angels on the mountaintops to sound the alarm.

As I mourned the unfathomable loss, a flicker of hope remained as stories spread of possible survivors emerging from beneath the water's weight.

For every death, could there not be a miracle to follow? I bargained with God underneath my breath. As if the miracles could somehow make up for the losses.

My faith was being tested, and a sense of urgency was stirring.

"Were we not all in danger of dying at any moment?" I soberly questioned. "Then what kind of life do I want to live?"

Providence

One night while I was working late at the photo shop, a young man with chocolate eyes and coffee skin wandered by my framing table. We'd met a time or two at church events. He was originally from Sri Lanka, but during a dangerous political conflict his family fled to Southern India. He now lived in Canada and worked as a carpenter. Suddenly, I put two and two together.

"Dan," I started, motioning for him to come back to my desk. "Is your family okay? Were any of them in the path of the tsunami?"

He was smiling as he meandered my way, so that was a good sign.

"The morning of the tsunami, my relatives were celebrating Christmas in the mountains," he explained. "If my cousins hadn't gone up to my aunt and uncle's place, who knows what could have happened?" he continued.

Dan went on to conclude his family's safety was providence, directed by God, and I agreed.

In the Old Testament, God had spared Noah and his family from a worldwide flood, and promised never to destroy the world in that way again. He sealed His word with a rainbow in the sky. Dan's relatives were spared. It was just the kind of miracle I was hoping to hear—just the kind of soul medicine I needed. But where was the ark for the others?

Surely no one really deserves to die? I found myself asking, despite what I knew the scriptures to say (Romans 5:12). Did the aftermath of the tsunami include a rainbow? And if so, what were the chances it would inspire survivors to trust in a loving God, while their neighbors lay in a watery grave?

By the time I got home, I was too weary to even think of writing, but my feet mysteriously plodded their way to the piano. My only solace was to rest my fingers on the keys and wait for God to send a message of comfort. Trivial selfish dreams and agendas were strangers to me now. Loving thoughts drifted to my almost grown, blue-eyed babies asleep in their beds. But who would comfort the dark eyed ones?

I wrote from a place of sorrow, unaware that my Faith Keeper was stirring my spirit, and lifting my head (Psalm 3:3).

Chapter Two
The Early Middle Years

Author

He sees the struggle; is it worth the trouble?
Loves you so much, to see you fall must hurt so bad.
Well He shares our pain, but won't take it away;
He knows glory comes on the final day.

So here's to the author and the finisher of your faith,
Put your past behind you, turn your eyes towards His face,
And climb those mountains, forge the oceans
To find your place; you will find your place.
If He is for you, who is against you?
You will find your place; you're gonna find your place.

So we keep on tryin'. Is it worth the cryin?
We pray all night and day and wonder why He waits.
Well He sees you grow, even though it seems slow;
In His plan so fine, we'll be ready on time.

> So here's to the author and the finisher of your faith;
> Put your past behind you, turn your eyes towards His face,
> And climb those mountains forge the oceans
> To find your place; you will find your place.
> If He is for you, who is against you?
> You will find your place; you're gonna find your place.

"Author" from *In View of His Mercy* ©1997/Cindy Palin

My husband was raised Anglican, and I Pentecostal. We got married in the Missionary church, because at the time it was the largest church in our area. Initially we planned to have a small wedding, and even considered having the reception at a restaurant, but my father wanted to invite the entire nation ... or so it seemed. My side had a ton of relatives.

"We're not going to follow tradition, are we?" Lloyd asked.

"What do you mean, exactly?" I replied.

"You know, where the family of the groom sits on one side, and the family of the bride on the other?"

I laughed and assured him that we didn't have to do any such thing.

Once married, we found the place to raise our future family at First Baptist Church. We made a distinct decision. If at all possible, we would commit and remain with one church, believing that this would help create a solid, steadfast foundation. Looking back, I'm convinced it was a decision inspired by the Holy Spirit, meant to help us learn about faithfulness. Remaining steadfast to one imperfect family is choosing to trust in

God's perfect will (Hebrews 10:24–25). We have been fortunate to serve and grow in the same church for many years—a church with a biblical mandate we can embrace.

The early years of child rearing were filled with the usual challenges of sleepless nights and finding breathing room in our quaint, four hundred square foot cottage. Although it was difficult to get to church on Sundays, we got there. For a while our church experience consisted of sitting in the nursery with a crying baby, then two, then three. How better to get to know other parents and their crying babies? Every once and a while, we even got to hear the preacher's message.

It was there that I learned what family should look like, or so I thought. Often it was painful. I would observe other families who seemed to have it all together, for generations, and compare them to my haphazard heritage. Periodically I asked myself if I even belonged there. At these times I would hear the author of my faith remind me to focus on Him and what He was doing in my heart.

A key part of His reminder was His choosing of me (1 Peter 2:9). As my faith roots grew, the Holy Spirit continued to affirm God's calling and purpose for my life. I began to understand through the power of the Holy Spirit that focusing on other families was actually an act of coveting and judgment. Was it my place to ask who had it together and who did not? Were we not all sinners, no matter what our outer wrappings portrayed, no matter where we came from (Romans 3:23)? Was God not able to use everything in our lives for his good (Romans 8:28)?

The author and finisher of my faith was teaching me to leave my past behind. My flesh and blood heritage did not define me. I was to fix my eyes on Him (Hebrews 12:2).

Chapter Three
Greener Grass

All I Have

If all I have is not enough, bring your love to mind;
If all I have is not enough, let me hear my children's cries;
If all of this still leaves me wanting,
Remind me of your sacrifice;
Bring the cross before my feeble eyes.

What could I ever want more than a Saviour's love?
The very reason that I live and breathe.
When will I ever learn that all I am to be,
Is nothing less than what He's planned for me?

If all I have does not compare, bring your love to mind;
The grass is greener over there, oh forgive my wandering eyes.
How can I say I live for you, Lord,
and want everything (security) money buys?
Bring the cross before my feeble eyes.

"All I Have" from *In View of His Mercy* ©1997/Cindy Palin

We faced some significant challenges in the first years of our marriage: an emergency delivery, epilepsy and asthma, and my parents' divorce, just to mention a few. Our church family rallied around us. Surrogate family members walked with us at every turn, and set examples of true love and faithfulness. I could see Jesus in their faces and their actions.

Through studying the Bible, I learned many vital truths that helped me get past unrealistic expectations. My spouse, friends, and family were not personally responsible for my happiness. When disappointed or confused, I learned to go to God. My faith was fuelled, and my mind refreshed. God continued to prove His faithfulness.

The elementary years found us one block south in a moderate sized house and homeschool-weary after a six-year commitment. My fatigue led to a dangerous bout of pneumonia, which in turn led us to enroll our children in a private Christian school just outside of town. That meant I would need to go to work outside the home. I didn't mind. I was grateful for the extra time I had with our children. Deep inside I sensed those years were going to count in the grand scheme of things. When I found employment, I was relieved to hear I could be home by the time the school bus rolled in.

We were like any middle class Canadian family with church on Sundays, our weekly work schedules, music lessons, basketball games, and competitions at the rink. I didn't see it coming … the fear and insecurity about our future. It wasn't for a lack of my Faith Keeper's warnings, as penned in the song "All I Have." He could see what was coming.

When the children were small, it seemed so easy to focus on what mattered most. As our family grew, the challenges got bigger. As our needs shifted, so did my faith. It happened so subtly, like the clouds momentarily hide the sun on a windy day. I began to worry. Worry festered, and my eyes drifted off my Saviour's love—not completely, but I no longer settled on His gaze. Instead, my circumstances took centre stage.

At first I was oblivious to my internal transition, so I don't suppose many noticed anything out of the ordinary from the outside. I began to entertain thoughts of securing our future on our own. We could reach our goals if we worked hard enough. Was it the striving or the goals that became problematic?

How do we know if the goals we are striving for are in line with God's will? I still believed Jesus was the way, but perhaps provision wasn't in His job description anymore? Or worse yet, maybe His supply was limited? Does my thinking process remind you of anyone in particular? Just call me Eve, the gal in the garden who just couldn't trust that God knew what He was doing.

Maybe my vow to follow Him meant I was expected to live like His disciples ... with one pair of sandals and a walking stick. How would my family respond to that kind of lifestyle? Looking back now, wallowing in worry about our future brought me to the proverbial fence. You know ... the one that draws a line between the green grass and the grass that's greener? This is where our will trumps God's will. This is where pride creeps in.

Let me stop for a moment. It wasn't that I had my eye on any one "thing" in particular. It wasn't that I had turned away from God completely, but my discontent and worry evidenced the fact that I'd decided God's plan wasn't good enough anymore. I thought if I could add to it, or supplement it, it would somehow be better. Suddenly, all He had done for me was not enough.

The harder I worked, the more I believed we could have our cake and icing too. The cake was my faith (main dish), and the icing (a little bit of the world) was slathered on the side. Unfortunately, when you bake that kind of a cake, the substance is always superficial.

As I came to a fork in the road, my Faith Keeper sounded a warning, yet I began writing my own recipe for success, despite what I knew scripture to say: "*'For I know the plans I have for you,' declares the Lord, 'plans to prosper you and not to harm you, plans to give you hope and a future'*" (Jeremiah 29:11).

Chapter Four
The Rescue Prayer

The Walking Dead

It's been a long and lonely night, a valley so deep,
Holding you oh so tight, while my knees bleed;
My lungs stopped breathing underneath the weight,
My heart stopped beating, hoping I could leave this place.

It's been a grueling uphill climb, a mountain so steep,
Following so close behind, intending to keep
Believing in the promises you make;
Expecting all or nothing lest you fade away.

Unless I can have your best I'm walking dead;
Imitation wings will never fly,
Unless I can see your face this life's a waste;
Rescue me or I will surely die.

"Walking Dead" from *My Heart's Lament* ©2010/Cindy Palin

Several Sundays in a row I found myself waiting for the sanctuary to empty so I could sit up front in the dark and stew. My "I can do it on my own" campaign was losing its fizz. I sensed there was something off balance in my life. I wanted something more ... but more of what? I analyzed my life, my faith, my church, and my marriage, and found I was unsatisfied. Not only were my husband and I tired, but everyone else looked tired, too. Everywhere I looked, relationships were strained, secondary, and dying. What was life suppose to be about again? What was this faith I professed? In the quiet, I heard God speak: "*Be still before the Lord and wait patiently for him*" (Psalm 37:7a).

"Great," I sighed with disdain, "two attributes I don't come by naturally."

In those sacred moments, a mental image appeared. I could see a human figure robotically moving forward on a steep inclined track. My fears and discontentedness, my lack of trust, and my "grass is greener" attitude had me trapped on a grueling uphill climb, a meaningless track of busy distraction.

And then it happened. Suddenly, while waiting for God, my spirit understood. I wanted more of Jesus! I wanted to recognize His face—not from a distance, but up close. I wanted to see His eyes wrinkle with laughter, and feel His breath warm on my face. I wanted to hear the unique inflections of my friend's voice. I wanted to press in so I could feel the heat radiate from His back as I followed close behind, to hear the sound of His footsteps ahead of me. No more wasting my time straddling the fence. I wanted God's best and nothing less.

I sensed the Holy Spirit remind me that he helps us in our weakness, and knows what to pray when we don't (Romans 8:26).

"Rescue me from the treadmill of life," I whispered, "and restore our relationship."

Another verse landed on my tongue, about restoring the years the locusts had eaten (Joel 2:25). Today I understand that verse to cover a broad spectrum. God mourned the disconnectedness of my youth. He mourned the brokenness that threatened my generation and the next, but if I were to surrender and trust Him completely, things could be different. New joy would replace the imitation wings I'd fashioned to reach the sky. The dreams He knew suited my family and I would come to fruition. I heard the Spirit emphasize prosperity of the soul, which comes with surrender and sacrifice, and is not about earthly gain. By embracing a new attitude of obedience, I would see evidence of Christ living in me (Proverbs 3:5–6, Psalm 37:4).

During this season a particular scripture took hold of my heart.

> *But make sure that you don't get so absorbed and exhausted in taking care of all your day-by-day obligations that you lose track of the time and doze off, oblivious to God. The night is about over, dawn is about to break. Be up and awake to what God is doing! God is putting the finishing touches on the salvation work he began when we first believed. We can't afford to waste a minute, must not squander these precious daylight hours in frivolity and indulgence, in sleeping around and dissipation, in*

> *bickering and grabbing everything in sight. Get out of bed and get dressed! Don't loiter and linger, waiting until the very last minute. Dress yourselves in Christ, and be up and about!*
> —Romans 13:11–14, MSG

The words leapt off the page as the remedy I'd been longing for. I'd been dozing off. I'd been losing perspective, heroically drowning in the day-to-day pressures of life. I was in danger of squelching His light, settling for the grey, and becoming the walking dead (which, by the way, was a phrase that arrived in my head long before the show by the same name appeared on television).

Let me be clear, Satan and his zombie appeal is far more attractive than how he's often portrayed. The damage he seeks to inflict is real, and is not at all represented by some fake makeup gore. On the other hand, as a believer I am to reflect the beauty of Christ in my face and lifestyle. I saw how easy it was to fall short. I didn't want to be a fake or a phony. I didn't want to play games with the gift of life He'd given, nor did I want to settle for going through religious motions. My soul began to hunger and thirst for Jesus in a new way.

Jesus, my Faith Keeper, was waking my spirit, rescuing me from becoming the walking dead, and reminding me of our covenant relationship and the abundant life He so wanted me to experience (John 10:10).

Chapter Five
Angry Laments

My Peace Flag's For Sale

I was inclined to seal my lips from cursing at the wind,
Tempted to trip on a few small words,
knowing what they meant;
Never was silence so over rated,
Never did sin look so good.

It crossed my mind to hold my tongue, and watch justice prevail;
I could have run but didn't move, my peace flag's for sale.
Never was silence so hard to come by,
Never did pain look so right.

So I took the bait, and I let them fly, to retaliate my love,
And I saw my faith sink in shifting sand and evaporate my love;
Never was silence so easy to shame,
And revenge tasted sweet.

"My Peace Flag's For Sale" ©2007/Cindy Palin

You've probably heard the saying, "be careful what you pray for." Several life altering events followed that rescue prayer. To our utter shock, my husband and I found ourselves unemployed. My beloved husband was devastated. His steadfast and faithful stewardship over a period of thirty-two years had earned my admiration and respect, as well as the respect of his peers and community. I had the privilege of working alongside of him for five of those years, and saw firsthand the joy his work and his co-workers brought to him. Could I dare entertain our situation was part of God's rescue plan? I believed God was not responsible for our new situation, but He could use it if we let Him.

This major change could have sunk our faith in the shifting sand. I won't divulge any details—out of love and consideration for all those involved—but I can honestly admit that my attitude of grace was not immediate. It developed over time, because of who the Spirit is inside of me.

At one point I enjoyed my angry lament at the piano and thought, *If King David can do it, so can I.* Thankfully the Holy Spirit turned my cursing to repentance. Those words of retaliation took flight on paper only, and I knew justice was possible only at the hand of my Faith Keeper.

While navigating through my husband's grief, I remembered a conversation we'd shared earlier that year.

"If you had the chance to do something different, what would it be?" I coaxed

There was a long pause, almost as if he hadn't heard me.

"I'd like to be involved in a short term mission of some kind, possibly building houses," he replied.

We'd met friends early on in our marriage, when I was singing at a sister church in Calgary, who had become involved in building projects in Nicaragua. The man's serious illness and miraculous healing led him and his wife to dedicate their lives to building housing for the poor. Obviously their transformation story made more of an impact on my husband than I had realized.

The Master Conductor

Within weeks of our earth shattering unemployment news, a longtime friend offered my husband a job in the carpentry business. Our friend made it clear that his request was sincere and not an act of charity. I understood that although my husband had no experience swinging a hammer, his managing skills and work ethic would be invaluable.

Meanwhile, our former employer turned "big box," and offered me a potential position in the freezer section, because the well known chain did not have a "framing department." I could see the irony despite the sting—an artist in the freezer.

"Well, that's certainly where the enemy of my soul wanted me," I smirked.

Perhaps framing art in our garage was more plausible.

I'd seen how retail had worn my husband thin. Changes in technology were threatening every traditional business in town. Why would I want to succumb to the same potential stresses? I strongly considered whether or not it was time for me to pick up my music dreams again and pour all my energies into writing and singing. With two of our teens still at home, another training in the city, and my husband facing a new career, I knew the "my" in our equation needed revisiting. Framing in the garage wouldn't guarantee a steady wage, but the return of previous clientele held promise.

One night before we truly settled on the "garage studio" idea, a phone call came. My husband's new employer suggested he and a team of carpenters come and insulate the garage. My heart plummeted at the thought of how much work it would take to rid ourselves of the typical garage paraphernalia. Moments later the phone rang again, and another family friend suggested he bring his entire family over to help clean out the garage. Did someone have an inside line to my thoughts? Absolutely! God doesn't miss a thing. Two back-to-back phone calls regarding our current discussion could not be a coincidence. I wasn't certain I was up for the retail challenge, but I didn't have to be—God was up to something. Could this also be part of His rescue plan?

For a couple of weekends in a row our driveway looked like an ant colony with people loading and unloading, and even "ants" stop to eat. The kitchen table was surrounded with neighbours, friends, and missionaries on furlough. Even my somewhat estranged father came to see what all the commotion was about. He was touched by our neighbours' generosity, and I was thrilled to have him join our party.

It was during one of these meals that I had the epiphany. God was answering both the rescue and the relationship elements of my prayer. Not only had the treadmill trap been sprung, but friends were popping up all over the place—friends we forgot we had. The sun was out, and the grass was green right in our own backyard. There was a peace flag flying boldly from His throne in my heart.

I could see my master conductor, smiling and orchestrating something new and beautiful for my husband and I (Revelations 21:1–8).

Chapter Six
The Seed of Hope

The Extra Mile

To believe in love is not enough
When you've seen what she's seen,
When you've lost what she's lost,
When you've been where she's been.
And do I want to feel her pain and let go and cry?
I just want to run away and believe a lie …

I don't have to do a thing,
Someone else can sure do better;
I don't want to see the truth,
Maybe I could just pray for her—now.
Gotta make you wonder, though, how
Sometimes love can't be shown
Without an arm around a shoulder,
Without a journey across a border.
Love, could be enough, when you go the extra mile.

> To believe in love is not enough
> When you watch someone die,
> And you know you'll die too.
> Not a thing you can do.
> So do I want to feel their pain, and let go and cry?
> I just want to run away and believe a lie
>
> I don't have to do a thing,
> Someone else could sure do better;
> I don't want to see the truth,
> Maybe I could just pray for her—now.
> Gotta make you wonder, though, how
> Sometimes love just can't be shown
> Without an arm around a shoulder,
> Without a journey across a border.
> Love could be enough—when you go the extra mile
>
> "The Extra Mile" © 2005/Cindy Palin

The Tsunami of 2004 was instrumental in opening my eyes again to the sanctity of life and the opportunity I had to think of others instead of just myself. More importantly, it served as a turning point in my life as the Holy Spirit began to draw me back to Kingdom priorities and to seek Christ first above all else, realizing there was plenty we could do to make a difference.

Following my conversation with Dan in 2004, he introduced me to a mission organization called Medic, which specialized in facilitating micro-loans in developing countries. While volunteering for Medic, I met many wonderful people, two of whom were Derek and Heather Liebenberg. Derek is Zimbabwean with Dutch roots. Heather is an Albertan from the Cochrane area. They met at Nazarene Theological College in Manchester, England. They married and were called to serve the widows and orphans of Bechuwandle, a suburb just outside the seaside village of Amanzimtoti, South Africa.

Derek would send updates to raise support for the Seed of Hope, which was established in 2003 as a multi-service community development centre, featuring stories of their new family. I opened the email and scrolled passed the pictures to read about the dark day two of Derek and Heather's friends were murdered. The young girl and her boyfriend had been regulars at the centre. The attackers raped and killed the young woman, then murdered her boyfriend. Derek went on to explain that the witch doctors in the area promoted rape as a cure for AIDS.

My eyes skimmed back up the page and rested on the young couple's photograph. Locking eyes with theirs kept them alive, at least on paper, but the blow of the barbaric injustice sent me curling into the fetal position. Nothing, not even my tears, could wash away thoughts of what their final moments must have been like. Again I found myself asking God, "Where were you?"

I clung to the story of Stephen in the book of Acts. Scripture tells us that while he was being stoned to death he looked up and saw Jesus sitting at the right hand of God, and then he fell asleep (Acts 7:54–60). Did these young people feel the presence of the Holy Spirit while the darkness violently ripped their light from this earth? I remembered that we are "struck down," but not destroyed (2 Corinthians 4:8). I wanted to hold them, but they were so far away, so I resigned to hold them in my prayers.

Had my grandmother's prayers conditioned my response? Did I really believe God would do something? Why would He now, when He hadn't intervened during the attack? As I prayed, I could see those still alive, mourning their loved ones, rocking back and forth in the dark. Their howling echoed underneath a moon we both shared.

"Holy Spirit, please sit with them among their ashes of despair," I cried.

Then I remembered Mary. I imagined her sitting in the dirt beneath the cross. She too had lost a child, having witnessed His crucifixion.

I understood. The Holy Spirit was reminding me that this was not the first time an egregious injustice had been committed on the earth. God's only son had suffered a horrible death at the hands of a blood-thirsty mob. He conquered death and rose to life on the third day so that those who believed would never be eternally separated from Him again. Before Christ ascended to the right hand of the Father, He promised that a comforter would come—the Holy Spirit (John 14:6).

"The Comforter is here," I whispered, knowing Him to be real in my life a thousand times over. I knew Heather and Derek's work at the Seed of Hope ensured many would come to know

Jesus and the new life only He could offer. They would be comforted. Even so, I stopped opening Derek's emails for a while.

Interpreting

With the letter and its contents still weighing heavy on my heart, I planned an escape—a visit to the movie rental shop. "The Interpreter" I read on the DVD, making a mental note of Nicole Kidman and Sean Penn. Perhaps a little entertainment would crowd out the reality of Derek's sobering message. How's that for a typical first world response?

Silvia Broome, played by Nicole Kidman, sits in her New York City apartment at her computer, waiting for a response from her brother in South Africa. The audience knows she isn't going to hear from him. The film opened with her brother, discovering a gruesome scene reminiscent of the Rwandan genocide, being shot and joining the ever-growing mound of dead bodies.

"So much for escaping reality," I winced. While the film isn't based on a true story, the content represents what has happened in our world a thousand times over.

We learn that most of Silvia's family was killed when she was a child. She and her brother are the only survivors. They take up arms against the corrupt government, but Silvia eventually trades her trust in weapons for words, and begins a job at the United Nations as an interpreter.

Despite the horrific pain of Derek's news and the movie's message, I felt the Holy Spirit moving me forward. I could hear the promise of words before I knew what they were. I believed in Christ's love amidst a very present evil, and I felt a profound truth was about to be stamped on my heart. I climbed the stairs once again to my music sanctuary and waited for God to speak. I too was an interpreter of sorts. I translated God's messages of love into song. By sharing songs inspired by His truth with others, even when it was difficult, I was living His love out-loud, whether I would cross a border one day, or a simple sidewalk.

Jesus, my Faith Keeper was calling my faith into action (James 2:17), and impressing upon my heart to go the extra mile. I could hear the Holy Spirit clarify that the extra mile was not a destination, but a decision—one we need to faithfully make each day.

Chapter Seven
Pity Party

More Than Enough

You know what it's like, because you've been here;
That reality won't heal my wounds (yes, it will—1 Peter 2:24).
And the truth declares that life is not fair;
Once again my heart remains unmoved;
There's a great big hole that comes and goes
When you lose someone you love,
And I have to beg for mercy, Lord.
Please be more than enough.

Keep me getting up each morning
When the rain won't leave my window;
Keep me serving you even if
You call everyone else home;
Keep me marching to a different drum,
'Cause hanging on is good for some;
But I desire the deeper stuff;
Please be more than enough.

> There'll be days when I will feel the darkness,
> When despair will dare to swallow me,
> And the words of friends will fall on deaf ears
> When the hand of sorrow covers me.
> There's a great big hole that comes and goes
> When you lose someone you love,
> And I have to beg for mercy, Lord,
> Always be more than enough
>
> "More Than Enough" ©January 18th, 2006/Cindy Palin

September's Indian summer couldn't entice my heart to sing, not this time. I slumped in a chair by the window and stared at the sky. I could see the rain waiting to pounce as soon as the blue curtain receded. My tears had long since crusted. How swiftly we forget the prayers we pray and the songs we sing.

I had just finished a call to my husband. He was at his new job and on lunch break. There had been another misunderstanding with some of our belongings at our old place of business, and I was confused. He couldn't make sense of it either, but he assured me he would try to help when he got home. On top of our employment change, we had been in the middle of a home renovation.

Some rescue, I dared to let my mind mutter.

The new windows had to be sent back. Would the raw floorboards bared beneath the linoleum be our hardwood stand-in for another seven years? The decision to re-insulate our old house had finally gotten underway, just to be put on hold. When our Canadian winter returned, Jack Frost would get to peek through our electrical outlets, again, and catch me feeling sorry for myself.

The ringing phone broke through my brooding and interrupted my pity party. I was shocked to hear Heather's voice from half way around the world. I couldn't fathom why she would be calling just out of the blue, and me of all people?

Come for a visit? Visit me? She barely knew me. I grabbed a piece of paper and a pen, half expecting to secure a date for sometime in the next year, only to hear...

"I'm in town," she announced.

Strong Dose of Perspective

Friends had pooled funds to get her back to Canada for a visit with her family, and some generous soul had even lent her a car. Moments later, or so it seemed, she was sitting at my table. I apologized for the rough, hewn floors, and cautioned her and Caleb to watch out for nails and staples. It seemed so surreal.

Not so long ago I'd been sitting at her kitchen table, listening about her struggle to keep their home. Derek, just forty years young, had died suddenly of a massive heart attack. He never got to meet their son.

My face flushed red. I don't recall to what extent I shared about our recent unemployment and renovation developments, but they paled in comparison. Yet as quickly as the thought reared its ugly head, a "God truth" response appeared. He didn't compare circumstances, and He didn't measure out love and grace on some invisible scale, otherwise why would He symphonize such a meet? God had a unique way of working and of bonding His people together.

Seeing Heather and Caleb, who was walking by now, was just what my heart needed—a warm, heavenly embrace, with a strong dose of perspective.

Heather and Caleb's lives were forever changed when Derek left the earth, as were all the lives of those he touched while he was living. The couple had heard the call to march to a different drum. Their "deeper stuff" was to be found in South Africa among the widows and orphans, but now she and her son were numbered among them.

After our visit I walked Heather and Caleb out to the car and waved goodbye to their flaxen blonde halos. Once back inside I couldn't help but revisit that fateful day, the day despair almost swallowed me whole.

"Derek's dead," the President of Medic announced over the phone that hollow December morning. It was the 28th, almost a year to the day when the largest tsunami recorded in history occurred, yet the hand of darkness threatened to pull us further under.

A Prayer Meeting

Derek and I first met at a Medic prayer meeting. The team was sitting in a circle in the middle of Dan's living room, and Derek was leading us in prayer for the many needs of the Centre.

As Derek prayed, my spirit twisted in turmoil. The needs were so great. What could my little family possibly do to help the Centre, or Medic, for that matter? I'd been volunteering on the side whenever I could, but contribute monetarily? Hardly. My husband and I were both working and raising our family. There wasn't much left over for us, much less to give away.

Derek continued to pray as I struggled to shut the door on my doubts. "Show me exactly what I can do, if anything," I pleaded under my breath.

In the midst of his prayer, I remembered the story he had shared earlier that day. A lady by the name of Ernestina had been struck down by a car, and to add insult to injury, her husband left her for the woman behind the wheel. She was now sewing at the Centre to make a living, but could sure use a new sewing machine. I knew what I needed to do. For years God had gently pressed me to get rid of distractions ... those extra hobbies that prevented me from doing His work effectively. This time the message was loud and clear, and made perfect sense.

Days after the prayer meeting I began organizing a fabric sale. The proceeds would go to buy Ernestina a new sewing machine. Effortlessly our community and church family rallied together, and pooled their sewing supplies as well.

During the sale preparations, I was asked to go to Africa with the Medic team. With my husband's permission, and much apprehension, I accepted their invitation and began planning for a February departure. With Derek suddenly taken from our midst, the Medic team experienced major difficulties and pulled out of the trip, but I knew I couldn't.

God hadn't necessarily called me to be a missionary overseas. God hadn't called me to suddenly leave my husband and three children behind. I could have just wired the funds to the Centre for them to buy a sewing machine, but God did insist He be first in my life. A visit to the Centre was a decision to look up and beyond my own needs and desires. It was a decision to put Jesus first again. I trusted He was going to show me new things. I prayed that as I drew nearer to Him, my children would too. I knew I'd gotten comfortable over the years. My faith had found a couch somewhere and sunk down in between the cushions for the long haul—nothing like a decision that would move me into complete reliance on Christ to get me out of my comfort zone! It wasn't until after I returned home that I noticed the connections, the threads my faith keeper had been weaving together for a long time.

In the 90s I'd been invited as a guest musician to the television show 100 Huntley Street. Heidi Baker, a well-known missionary to Mozambique, was a guest on the same show. After the taping we all met for lunch. Heidi looked at me across the table and said, "You should come to Africa." I knew better than to respond with a flat out "no," because God has a sense of humour. Deep down I wanted to tell her I was afraid, that maybe my faith wasn't big enough for that kind of trip, but I had another sincere objection. Why did everybody think they had to go to Africa to help God? Were there not plenty of walking wounded right in my own backyard?

A Miracle a Day

I cried like a baby when we got to the security gate. It must have been excruciating for my husband. I could see the agony on his face.

"I thought you wanted to go?" he agonized.

I nodded my head, but couldn't speak.

"So why are you crying?" he asked.

I couldn't' tell him I was afraid. I let go of his hand and pushed through the gate, careful not to look back.

Family friends had advised me to look for a relative of theirs that was supposedly on the same flight. That hope kept me from running back into my husband's arms. I never did find her, but I kept my journal close by, determined to watch for, and write down, one miracle a day.

If the long trip to London seemed void of joy, the approach and the airport drained me dry. First, our plane had to circle several times above Heathrow before there was a runway available to land on. Once we touched down, a maze of construction masked our view of anything that may have resembled an air terminal, let alone the city of London. Boarding a bus to get to another building was a new one for me, but to my relief they knew what they were talking about. Someone on the plane had told me I'd have plenty of time to see the sights before my next flight, so my feeble legs got to the escalator, which led to the "tube."

"Where are you off to?" an official asked while checking my itinerary.

"I was told I had time to see Windsor Castle," I replied nervously.

"That's a negative, Mom. You'll miss your next flight if you leave the area," he directed.

Was that a "mom" or a "ma'am?" I wondered curiously, then smiled at the sound of his pleasant British accent.

"Better head on back the way you came. I'm sorry," he directed, and handed me back my papers.

I wove my way through more construction and discovered a wide retail corridor that resembled the civilized world. I found a place to eat, only to get lost when I heard the final boarding call. Asking for help in "English" doesn't guarantee a response. Pointing towards the escalator was about all the airport personnel could muster. So up I went.

"So much for a miracle here," I sighed, disgruntled with the lack of hospitality.

While boarding the plane to Johannesburg, I noticed a large group of people filing in behind me. They all sat down in close proximity, until I was completely surrounded. It was comforting to discover they were nurses and doctors with medicine on their way to an orphanage in Mozambique. It was their third or fourth trip.

Not only were they wonderful company, but they also instructed me on several important details for landing in Johannesburg, one of which was removing my jewelry. Twelve hours later when we deplaned, they strongly suggested I stay with their group through security. The men carried my luggage past armed guards, and never left my side until we had to separate at our different departure gates. "Miracle number one," I jotted down. "I didn't have to travel alone."

The hot tarmac mixed with Durban's arid atmosphere had flattened my lungs like pancakes. Besides the struggle to breathe, there was the other real dilemma of searching for the person who was going to be picking me up. Although I had communicated faithfully with the Centre for months, asking all the pertinent questions, response from their end had been sparse. I didn't have a clue who to look for, and had no idea how my driver would know who I was. Thinking about that moment now makes me laugh. I couldn't have been hard to spot, with my "deer in the headlights" expression.

Eventually a friendly gentleman waved my way. His words were swallowed up by the noise of the crowd, but I recognized the unique timbre of his voice. I smiled and allowed him to help me with my luggage. We weaved our way to the parking lot through a swarm of bodies, heat, and pungent smells. He threw my suitcases in the back of a little truck and motioned for me to get inside. To my surprise, I couldn't stop grinning. He sounded just like Derek.

"I'm Abe," he said as he reached out his hand for a shake.

"I'm Cindy," I responded, shaking his hand. "You must be Derek's dad."

He nodded and turned the key.

"I'm sorry for your loss," I blurted out right away, as a lump formed in my throat. I don't recall his exact response, and we rode in silence for a brief time along the coastal highway, which shouldered the Indian Ocean.

The physical beauty surrounding me did nothing to capture my attention as much as the Holy Spirit that day, as I noted how God carries His wounded. Otherwise, how could Abe function? He'd just lost his son, yet he was willing to do some mundane chore like drive to the airport to pick up a stranger. Abe was not unfamiliar with loss, I reminded myself, as stories of his family's escape from Zimbabwe resurfaced in my brain. Obviously God was more than enough for Abe.

I tried to blink back my tears and noted another miracle. This is the way God loves. He gives, and He takes away, and then gives some more (Job 1:21), shaping His family from bits of tender, broken pieces around the world (Psalm 51:17), into one mighty heartbeat.

The tiny tin truck stopped outside the gated Strandburg. The blue block of a building stood stoically on the sand, a few hundred feet from the ocean's lair. Abe spoke into a security intercom, and the gate opened for him to drive through. Next we climbed three flights of stairs to a barred apartment door, where I would be staying for the next month.

An Irish accent greeted me, and Abe waved goodbye. Elspeth motioned me inside with her warm smile to a cool ocean palette of blue and green. To my surprise, three young people, very close in age to my own band of three kids back home, sat visiting in the living room while listening to the sounds of Abba. For a fleeting second I felt like I'd simply crossed the street, as my kids had been playing the same music when I left for the airport.

Instantly I noted a kitchen to the right with running water, and a bathroom to the left with a working toilet. This was a far cry from a mud hut, I concluded. Miracles were multiplying now at quite a fast rate. Was I mistaken, or had God really gone out of His way to make me feel welcome?

Once the young people left, everything grew very quiet. Although my roommate was in close proximity, a hollow feeling of loneliness settled in like the fog swoops in from the sea. It would be three days before we were picked up and taken to the Centre, and longer before we got a ride to buy groceries. I spent those first few days on foreign soil crying with my face pressed to the musty carpet. The angry rain and the ocean's growl mocked my arrival. I could hear a faint voice singing, "Keep me getting up each morning when the rain won't leave my window." I didn't think I'd need to heed my own medicine.

Bitter Sweet Blessings

We arrived at the Centre and had to buzz to get in through a fairly un-daunting locked gate. We walked across a yellowed yard to a barred entrance, which revealed a pale, painted brick foyer. Once inside, we were directed down a hall lined with rows upon rows of barred gates and windows. It was cold and sterile, and nothing like the picture a dear friend had shown me from the Centre's grand opening a year prior. The flowers were gone. The grass had dried up, and there was no one smiling on the steps to greet us. Derek's death had come, and death had lingered ... everywhere.

I could hear voices coming from the north end of the hall, and was relieved to find a room full of smiling faces across the threshold. Morning worship and prayer were about to start, so I quickly sat down on the first empty plastic chair I could find. I began to shiver and noticed the windows had no glass in them. The morning breeze was free to play with our hair and blow through our sweaters, but it was a far cry from a Canadian cold. It seemed we were the last to arrive, so as soon as we got seated the singing began. Without warning, a fountain of tears erupted. I was a mess.

I've always been spiritually sensitive to the language of music, but hearing their sacrifice of praise coming from such rich, velvet voices rendered me helpless. I'd crossed a border alright, but never expected to be the one needing someone's arms around my shoulders. I found myself considering another border some two thousand years ago, a border too profound for any mind to fathom—Jesus passing through Heaven's portal to a dusty manger stall for me.

Ernestina got her sewing machine—two, in fact. Today, I know the Centre offers a four level sewing program, as well as many other specialty training and service programs. Slowly we got to paint and plant, but mostly we were given the gift of togetherness and family. What a bittersweet blessing to be allowed a part in those fragile months following Derek's death. God had certainly outdone Himself in the miracle department as far as I was concerned.

One of the most palpable miracles played out a couple of days before I flew home. Secretly, the entire time I spent in South Africa was underlined with the longing to visit Derek's grave. He had died in December, and my trip to the Centre took place the following February. I kept childishly thinking that if I could just get there, then I'd know for certain he wasn't coming back. I never said a thing to anyone, because I knew travelling to the cemetery was no small feat. I'd been told that right after Derek's funeral the Centre's van had been stolen. Spar, a wonderful volunteer at the Centre, was using the only jeep they had to transport sick people to the hospital. To say transportation was limited was an understatement. I was aware there were plenty of people who knew Derek at a deeper level that should be granted the privilege to visit his grave, over and above me.

Missionaries Carl and Michelle Waldron, who were staying a couple of floors below me at the Strandburg, called me one morning with a question.

"Would you be interested in coming with us to the cemetery?" Carl asked. They had a rental car, which had room for four.

"We'd like to take Heather, and there's room for you too," Carl stated matter of factly.

I was humbled, and momentarily at a loss for words.

"Carl, I would love to come," I finally answered, "but only if you're sure there is no one else that should be going." There was no way to convey how incredibly moved I was, and how grateful to God, who knows my heart's every desire.

The Deeper Stuff

The car turned into the cemetery and wove its way down a road with a canopied sky. The trees seemed taller here, less tropical, and more forested. The sun played hide-and-seek through the leaves, and danced on the rim of my glasses. *How odd*, I scowled, *for death to come, and the sun to shine.* To my horror, garbage lay everywhere—mostly remnants of liquid hope in a bottle.

Death ... a good reason to drink, my heart empathized.

My mind drifted to the chatter about the danger in these parts. Apparently graveyards in Africa are a robber's paradise.

A more predictable pairing, I ached. *Depravity and despair.*

My eyes turned towards the front seat where Carl sat behind the steering wheel. He was tall and safe and very knowledgeable about our surroundings. Many people, including myself, had commented on how he looked as though he was a native South African. Would his stature help if a scuffle developed here in the cemetery? *Nothing but God's protection would really cut it, if indeed trouble found us*, I concluded.

I was inches away from a painful reality and still a hopeless romantic, believing my God cared and was in complete control. I just didn't understand it all.

The tires quietly rolled to a stop, as if they knew we were on hallowed ground. We somberly climbed out and locked the doors behind us. The doors clicking shut, the gravel crunching beneath our feet, and the noisy birds overhead, irreverently assaulted my ears.

"Could everyone just be quiet," I wanted to scream out loud.

I followed Heather up a gentle slope to a clearing. She bent down slowly and knelt in the soil, resting her folded hands on her pregnant tummy. My eyes quickly diverted to the ground.

Keep yourself together, my scrambled thoughts said.

The soil was a strange colour. Must have been the clouds casting their shadows. Heather began to pluck weeds and smooth out the ground with her hands. I looked closer and saw a simple cross, made of sticks, and could hear someone say there hadn't been time to get a proper monument made yet. It was a terrible sight. It was all wrong somehow. It had to be a mistake.

Part of my mind slipped away to a tomb from another place and time. I could hear the sisters scolding Jesus for taking too long to come to their brother's aid. Now he was dead, and Jesus was too late to save him (John 11). I wanted to scold Jesus right then and there for allowing my brother, Derek, to die.

Then I recalled how Jesus spoke sweet Lazarus from the grave. I believed Jesus could raise anyone from the dead, anytime, anywhere, but for some reason, unknown to us on this side of eternity, our Lazarus would not be returning. Then my thoughts turned to the disciples. I imagined the emptiness the band of brothers felt, leaving their once very much "alive" Messiah dead and buried in another tomb. They were left behind. Again, I recalled Christ's promise of a comforter (John 14).

"Holy Spirit, please comfort us," my spirit pleaded.

Carl broke the silence.

"Would you like to sing that song you wrote?" he asked.

I knew instinctively I would never forgive myself if I didn't try. A father and son, a husband, friend, and leader had been taken from us, and somehow we all had to move forward.

I nodded to Carl and straightened my shoulders. I opened my lips to form the words, only to hear a faint little girl's voice begin to sing. The raindrops that had been on hold nearby now fell on cue.

Derek isn't coming back, is he Lord? my mind acknowledged in between the lyrics. *And this time, we're the ones left behind.*

I continued to sing defiantly, no matter what I sounded like. I sang for my friends and for myself, but most of all for Heather, and the future. I sang for the Lord as a sign of my allegiance, even if He called everyone else home. I sang to silence the enemy of my soul. Soberly, I sensed the song would be instrumental in ushering forward other losses and victories to come. But despair would not swallow me. Sorrow did not get the last word. Jesus, my Faith Keeper was allowing me the privilege of sharing in his sufferings and rejoicing in His future glory (1 Peter 4:12, 13).

Chapter Eight
Seasons

Slim to Nothin'

Slim to nothin' worn down to a thread;
Slim to nothin' but not quite dead;
Well, that's the best place to be;
Broken and raw,
That's the best place to hear the voice of God ...

... Slim to nothin', scraped down to the bone;
Slim to nothin', lost and alone;
Well, that's the best place to be;
Humbled and flawed,
That's the best place to hear the voice of God ...

Cause when you hear him,
Chances are you're near him,
And when you're near him
You belong.
Yeah when you hear him,
Chances are you're near him,

> And when you're near him,
> You belong.
>
> Slim to nothin', weak and he is strong;
> Slim to nothin', singing his song;
> Well, that's the best place to be;
> Centred and awed,
> That's the best place to hear
> The voice of God ...

"Slim to Nothin'" from *My Heart's Lament* ©2010/Cindy Palin

We sat on a slope of tinder dry moss outside the condo, which faced the marina's outstretched skeletal hand. Its bare bones floated on the surface of the shimmering lake, with only a few bobbing boats still captured in its grip. The autumn sun was pulling the shade, blotting out the trees and cabins on the other side of the water, smudging everything in blue shadow.

"The end of a season marks the beginning of another," I bravely told myself.

But with our son leaving home at the age of sixteen, I was afraid winter would come and stay forever. I glanced to my left to see his hands admiring a petrified piece of driftwood, scraped down to the bone.

"Mom, do you think we're actually going to find a place for me to stay?" he questioned, nervously tapping the stick on the ground.

I motioned for him to pass the wood to me, and ran my fingers down its smooth surface, noticing its twists and turns and knots—like the one in the pit of my stomach. Undoubtedly, he had one too.

"I'm trusting God will lead us in the right direction," I answered.

We had one week to find him a school and room and board, so he could pursue his dream of skating under a Calgary coach. The decision had been excruciatingly difficult to make—one we never would have considered had it not been for his drive and determination. He had the skill and the personality to be an athletic performer, and had been making some promising contacts on his own. The chances of us making it happen were slim to none. How could all his needs be met in such a short time? As I contemplated our next step, I found myself reflecting on Africa once again.

God's Economy

Getting in touch with loved ones back home had been difficult for me. My best alternative was the landline in the main office of the Centre, which wasn't always available. With the time change, it was best for me to call in the late afternoon, which was when they usually sent us home and locked the gate. It was in everyone's best interest to be out of the suburb by 4:00 p.m. at the latest, before it got dark.

One particular afternoon I was able to get through to my husband back home for a brief review of how everyone was doing. To my surprise our son and some other skaters from the same club had been given the opportunity to participate in the World Figure Skating Championship opening ceremonies. I was thrilled to hear the good news, but couldn't imagine what that meant for my husband without me home to help. His willingness to allow me to go to the Centre added the role of chief cook and taxi driver to his already demanding job at the photo-shop.

To my relief, he told me that another skater's family had stepped in to help by offering our son a bed closer to the city and transportation to and from practices. I couldn't help but conclude it was God's economy at work. Not that my travelling to Africa meant God owed me something. Not that my desire to follow Jesus meant everything should go smoothly, but I sincerely believed God cared about every detail. Knowing the stress on my little family was alleviated somewhat, I felt free to finish my month long commitment at the Seed of Hope.

A couple of weeks after the informative call, I found myself sitting in the Strandburg apartment with Heather, who was delicately picking out my tangled extensions. I'd hoped to surprise the kids with an authentic African hairdo, but the itch had outlived its welcome. As each unwoven strand fell to the floor, I found myself thinking of Derek and Heather's dreams, and how they had seemingly fallen apart. At the same time, I couldn't stop believing that God was more about weaving dreams together.

The very woman who had stepped in to help our family back home was Heather's best friend. Heather and Derek lived in Canada for a time after they married and met Tracey and her husband there. Eventually, God called Derek and Heather to Africa. Time passed and tragically Tracey's husband, who was a policeman, was driving to work early one morning and was struck and killed by an oncoming vehicle.

Months before my arrival in Africa, I bumped into Tracey in the mall as I was gathering last minute items for my trip. We'd shared many a cold bench in various ice rinks over the past several years, yet it was during our brief chat at the shopping centre where I first learned of the couples' close friendship. I was amazed at how closely we were connected and didn't even know it.

Tracey shared her grief over Derek's death and relayed her desire to visit Heather at the Centre one day. She asked me to give Heather greetings on her behalf, and I was all too happy to do so, but I was bewildered at why things happen the way they do. Both women had lost their husbands. Based on their history, their close friendship, and their tragic loss, Tracey should have been going instead of me. Instead, I got to embrace a community on the other side of the world, while she and her family embraced my son.

My thoughts drifted to Heather and her unborn son. My concern for my family back home paled in comparison to Heather's situation. One moment I was meditating on God's amazing provision for my little family back home, and the next I was aching for Heather and the son she would soon introduce to this world.

I wondered what it was all about. I wasn't sure what God was trying to teach me would all make sense right away, but the faithfulness displayed all around me by those who were suffering, and still choosing to believe, was invaluable. I trusted the experiences both past and present would continue to bring clarity to my faith journey and relationships further down the road.

No sooner had I laid the driftwood down when my son picked it back up and motioned as if he were going to break it.

"No, don't," I interrupted quickly, as if the stick and I were connected, as if I might break as well.

"I want to keep it. Nothing like a souvenir to remember this moment," I smiled weakly, trying to imagine a future less raw.

"Your dad and I are asking God to help us find a suitable place for you to live," I continued, noting his furrowed brow.

His fair eyebrows were just starting to appear on his forehead, right underneath a swath of striking reddish-blonde hair. Memories of his little red head and large blue eyes playfully peeking outside of a cardboard box materialized. Those eyes and mischievous grin were destined for adventure.

God answered our prayers. He doesn't always clearly confirm, but a door opened and we walked through it. A friend from my high school days lived in the city, not far from the rink and the sports school our son was enrolled in. She even had a son the same age. If it hadn't been for her organizing our high school reunion earlier in the summer, I never would have thought to call her. I distinctly remembered what she said during one of our catch-up chats: "If there's anything I can ever do …"

We got home from our rare weekend in the mountains and I called her. We set up an interview, and the rest is history.

Tearing of the Soul

I was relieved to know that our son had a home away from home, but his leaving marked another lesson on the tearing of the soul. Half of my heart lived at home with my husband and our two daughters, while the other half rode around in our son's pocket somewhere. Often I would stand on the back step and wave goodbye to my girls as they left for school. As they got in the neighbour's car, I would imagine myself standing at a city bus stop, watching our son get on a bus. Whenever I was driving somewhere in town, I would turn on the city traffic report. I'd look at the clock and make a mental note of what part of the city our son might be in at that exact time.

The months passed, and I told myself I was getting the hang of my heart beating in two places. My body language may have fooled most people, but I knew, and God knew, that I was worn down to a thread. Children aren't supposed to leave home until they're finished school, as a rule. One of mine had left the nest prematurely, and this mother bird was not coping well. Something told me that when the time came for our daughters to leave home, it wouldn't be any easier.

I once questioned how Jesus could relate to a mother's pain of separation. Then the Spirit quickly reminded me that the disciples were Christ's children. When Jesus had to leave the earth, He had to leave His children behind. He knew the Holy Spirit, the Comforter, would follow, and that His children would be comforted and equipped.

"O Holy Spirit," I whispered, "you are a busy guy."

My usual prayer regiment multiplied, which by the way isn't always a good sign. Repetition can sometimes be a sign of less trust. Oh, how God is patient with our whining and begging! Since that time I have practiced praying scripture over my family. No matter how I pray, I am humbled that my Faith Keeper hears me.

There are other crutches we lean on at times as a substitute for Jesus. A rich bodied red wine became a new staple in my cupboard. For a while I justified it by calling it the latest in foodie trends.

"It's the culture; it's all about the fancy glass," I said.

But if you can't say no to just one drink, then "fancy" soon becomes a cover up for "foolish." I knew deep down inside the wine was a substitute for Jesus. Rather than trusting Him with everything, I was numbing everything. When I found myself reaching for a glass in the middle of the afternoon, I became discouraged with my flawed nature. The Holy Spirit helped me understand that the more dependent I was on other substances for comfort, the less I could hear His voice, and I wanted to hear Him. I needed to be near Him, as close as a little girl snuggled in underneath her father's arm.

Our family seemed to adjust, but I've come to realize that we all experienced a type of separation anxiety in one way or another. At night I had the most difficulty. I thought darkness meant silence, but that's where your fears and failures find their voice, if you let them. Instead of counting sheep, I would try to recite scripture.

Do not be anxious about anything, but in every situation, by prayer and petition, with thanksgiving, present your requests to God. And the peace of God, which transcends all understanding, will guard your hearts and your minds in Christ Jesus.

—Philippians 4:6–7

To this very day, every time the darkness rolls in I remind myself of who I belong to. I pull the covers up to my chin like a child and imagine where each of our children are, then pray for the Holy Spirit to be near them, like an angel standing guard. Now that they are all grown and live away from home, I no longer have the privilege of tucking them in, but no one can take away the privilege of praying for them.

The petrified wood our son found that late September still sits on our mantel. I smile as I think of the word "petrified," which means both fear and preservation. I was petrified with fear at first, but Christ's sacrificial love preserves me.

Our children like to tease me about that "stupid stick," pretending to drop it, or hiding it in precarious places. The crooked stick shouts, "He can make our path straight," if we'll let Him (Proverbs 3:5, 6). We will experience all kinds of change and loss in our life, but Jesus will never leave us or forsake us (Deuteronomy 31:6). As I drew near to my Saviour during the winter of my faith, my Faith Keeper drew near to me.

Chapter Nine
An Angel Moves In

Keeping the Faith

We'll be the song, He is the voice;
You are the hands, and we made a choice
To carry our cross, where ever we go;
Keeping the faith until we get home.

We'll say the prayers the Spirit brings;
You'll lift the hearts of the suffering;
Together we'll love, the lost and alone;
Keeping the faith until we get home.

Keeping the faith, fighting the fight,
We'll run the race into the night;
And long down the road when our hearts break,
We'll finally know the Keeper of Faith.

"Keeping the Faith" ©July16, 2002/Cindy Palin

Our eldest daughter was in grade twelve when my husband suggested we consider offering room and board to a college student. It made sense to choose our son's room, as he lived away, and the extra money would help with skating costs.

"Do you remember the gal who use to live in Olds?" my husband began. "She went to Olds College and attended our church," he continued. "I heard she's moving back, something about taking on a leadership position with Intervarsity Christian Fellowship."

I remembered Katie alright—her fierce love for God and people, her gift with horses, and her love of music. She was a country girl from the prairie, with a glow of Heaven's light in her hair.

"Are you suggesting she might want to live here?" I queried, with a bit of an edge to my tone. "I'm sure she has plenty of other prospects," I quipped, not meaning to shut his ideas down, but shutting them down just the same. Something inside of me didn't quite feel qualified to live with an angel.

A couple of days after our discussion, I began to feel convicted. Who's to say my husband's idea wasn't guidance from God? I didn't have Katie's number, so I did the next best thing. I moved forward, leaving the selection process up to God.

I reached for the phone and called the Student Residence office. Within an hour there was a room and board ad on their bulletin board, and a notice online as well. That was a Monday. Wednesday the phone rang.

An Angel Moves In • 57

"Hi, I'm calling about the room and board ad," a cheerful voice announced.

"Well, hello," I responded nervously, wondering if I was ready to share our home with a stranger.

"May I make an appointment to come by and have a look at the room?" she asked.

"Are you in town today?" I replied.

"No, I'm still in Saskatchewan, but I'll be in town on Friday, and was hoping to line up a couple of leads," she said.

"You sound so familiar," I admitted curiously.

"You too," her voice radiated through the phone.

"How did you get our information, if you're still in Saskatchewan?" I asked

"A friend of mine walked into Frank Grisdale Hall yesterday and saw a slip of paper on the bulletin board. She knew the requirements you posted fit me to a tee, and called me right away with your number."

All of the sudden I put two and two together. God has such a sense of humour.

"Are you Katie ... Katie Housek?" I blurted in surprise.

"Yes, I am," she replied, "but how do you know me?"

I laughed with relief and explained how we had met at church when she lived in Olds. After a short discussion, she knew exactly who we were as well, and an interview was set for the following Friday.

"See you then," I chided, certain God was smiling.

To this day most people believe Katie came to lead Intervarsity, and she did and went above and beyond the call of duty, but I'll always know a large part of her arrival was divine intervention. She was a divine gift leant to my family and I during a difficult time. She was an extension of God's hands helping me navigate through the spring of reawakening and the fall of separation, and the storms inbetween.

History records God assigning angels to a variety of tasks. Katie was my warrior angel, with a sword at her side. We didn't know it when she moved in, but we were destined to engage in some heavy-duty spiritual warfare.

The morning she arrived we spent more time praying together than anything else. She decided there was no reason to check out the other place on her list. She was home.

I'd never heard someone tell Jesus they loved him, like she did, faithfully at the end of every prayer. It made me wonder: Do I love Jesus? I believe, but do I love Him? In faith I began to end my prayers just the way she did.

"I love you, Jesus."

It soon became apparent to me that by pledging my love I was actually making a choice to love, regardless of how I felt, and regardless of my circumstances. I was making a choice to trust Jesus and respond to His every word. I was amazed at how that truth applied to every aspect of my life, and as I chose to speak love out, my Faith Keeper began shaping obedience and faithfulness into my character.

Our angel clad in armour stayed for two years, and during that time God used her to solidify relationships. I knew for certain she was an intricate answer to the second part of my rescue prayer. She was my prayer partner, sister, and friend, as well as big sister to our daughters and son. My husband was privileged to expand his fatherly role as well, gently intervening when Katie's hectic pace needed reigning in.

When our eldest daughter went off to University, Katie and our youngest formed a special bond. Again, I could see my Faith Keeper at work, even in the Bible study she began hosting at our house on Tuesday nights. Twelve or so girls from the college would gather in our home, and Katie would organize a dinner based on a menu from another part of the world. We would enjoy our meal together and then dig into God's Word.

Her first spring with us was packed full of mission preparations for the summer. She had already been to Mongolia once, and was planning to return again at the end of the school year. We shook our heads when she told us one roll of toilet paper would have to suffice for the entire summer. Stories of her bathroom escapades kept us in stitches ... finding rocks to hide behind only to be discovered by nomadic shepherds—who were just as accustomed to seeing bare bottoms on the tundra as they were to seeing sheep.

We sat on the couch together one evening and began discussing her upcoming trip. One of Katie's specialties was evangelism. She wanted everyone she met to know Jesus. Her physical strength, her education, and her love of singing and writing music on her guitar were all used to underline the message of the Gospel.

"If something happens to me," she said, "I wouldn't mind 'Keeping the Faith' sung at my service."

I shifted my position and turned to lock eyes with hers.

"What on earth are you talking about?" I asked with a panicked tone, but knowing very well what she was getting at.

Her first summer in Mongolia had not been exempt from danger, and she was merely preparing herself, and me, for the reality of missionary life in a hostile environment. She'd told me of the attack on her life the previous year, and I teared up at the thought of this world losing the unique light her faith and courage offered.

"When did you write this song?" Katie inquired, as she walked to the piano and picked up the sheet music. It was one of a rare few I had actually finished scoring.

My eyes looked for the copyright date, but instead settled on the dedication line. I'd almost forgotten about another boarder who had warmed our hearts some ten years prior.

Long Down the Road

In our early years of marriage, a young man had come to live with us while attending Bible College in a nearby town. His first year of college was graced with a lovely girl, which I'm told caused him endless frustration because he had made a vow to God not to date right away. The letters he pecked out on our computer keys told me it was only a matter of time. Not that I read them, but it was how he talked about her, how he floated around so helplessly distracted.

He ended up moving and finishing college, and eventually we were invited to their wonderful wedding. Early on in their marriage they accepted a mission post. On one of their furloughs home, I noticed something unusual. Our friend's wife was playing a game on the living room floor with our children, but her usual sweet demeanour had all but disappeared. I'd never seen her this way, and knew something was wrong.

They returned to their posting then home again. I couldn't wait to see them, but still felt strangely unsettled. Just as my grandmother had been prompted by the Spirit to pray for me as a child, I felt as if God was prompting me to pray for our friends. It wasn't long before I found myself back at the piano writing a message I believed was specifically for them.

Through different reliable sources, I heard that the organization they were working with was experiencing some heart wrenching challenges. On top of that, our friend had taken very ill—not once, but several times. Thankfully he was well again. *What mission assignment is problem free?* I argued with myself. *Especially one with major cultural differences and life size mosquitoes?* But as I began to write, my heart felt strange ... as though the real storm was just beginning.

Our church family planned to have a send off for our friends at an upcoming Sunday service before they left for another term. It was the right place to share the new song God had given, but I wasn't sure I should be the one to suggest it. Instead, I kept silent and asked God to bring confirmation.

One afternoon while I was going about my outdoor chores, I looked up to see our friend's beautiful wife walking up our driveway. Instantly my heart leapt inside of me. Could it be my confirmation had arrived?

"Well, hello there," I chirped. "To what do we owe this visit?"

"You're going to think this is a bit strange," she admitted, as she made her way onto our back step.

I smiled with anticipation.

"You don't happen to have a song that you could sing at our service this Sunday?" she asked.

"As a matter of fact," I started, "I believe I do."

Neither one of us knew that day what lay ahead—that the "long road" and "heartbreak" in the lyrics would actually come true. Our friends had gone to lift the hearts of the suffering, only to come home with a renewed understanding of what it means to share in Christ's suffering, and what it's like to fight against principalities and powers who seek to shred our faith into millions of tiny ineffective pieces. Thanks be to God that despite the enemy's attack on their marriage, they remained faithful.

Today I know the song prayer wasn't just for them, but for those of us who form the church of Jesus Christ—the family of God. God was showing me how we are all intricately involved in mission together. There are those who go and those who stay behind, but we are of one mind and spirit. Together we love the lost and alone, and desire to be faithful until Jesus calls us home. Together we respond to the prompting of the Holy Spirit and show up in one another's lives. We lift one another up in prayer. We cry and laugh together. We pick each other up. We cheer each other on. We speak God's truth into one another's lives and ask Him to make us the examples we need to be for our brothers and sisters. We keep the faith, fight the fight, and share His good news (the Great Commission) together (Matthew 28:16–20).

The Prayers the Spirit Brings

Katie had left on her trip with the mission team under the umbrella of MB missions. I stood cupping my coffee beneath my chin so the steam could tickle my face awake. Soaking in the rich aroma spurred my thoughts towards Katie's meagre "physical" reality: her backpack, her dried food, and her one roll of toilet paper. I looked around my warm kitchen and pictured her team shivering around a campfire with a kettle over the flames.

"Oh Lord, I'm sure glad you didn't call me to Mongolia," I sighed with relief.

Suddenly, a wave of something swept over me. I knelt right then and there on the linoleum floor. I couldn't get Katie out of my mind. Was I supposed to pray? Another wave swept over me, and I began to weep uncontrollably. I tried to speak, but didn't know what to say. Again I was reminded of how the Spirit knows what to pray when we don't. The tears kept coming, and I wondered what time it was in Mongolia, and where Katie might be at that exact moment. I opened my mouth to pray, and then the phone rang.

"Hello," I stammered, trying to sound somewhat collected.

"Cindy?" a far away voice called.

"Katie?" I responded in shock.

"I need you to pray," she announced amidst a cloud of white crackle.

"How are you able to call me?" I asked in amazement.

"We've got a Satellite phone," she reminded me, and I remembered how her team talked of getting one for their trip.

"Katie," I answered, "you're not going to believe this, but the Holy Spirit has already brought me to my knees. What's going on?"

"It's late," she began. "We've had a ... a long day."

I tried to wrap my mind around what a long day meant for Katie and her team. How many miles had they hiked on foot? How many mountains had they climbed? She sounded weary but excited at the same time. I looked at the clock and did the conversion. It was midnight there.

"What's the noise in the background?" I questioned, hoping she could move to a quieter place so I could hear her better.

"I'm in my tent; the wind is crazy. Cindy, there's a woman who needs our help."

My ears began to separate the white noise. I could make out the flapping of her tent.

"She may be involved with demonic spirits," she continued. "We're going to need people to pray with us. We've called a couple of others to pray as well. I've got to go ...," her voice trailed off. "Love ya."

Instantly, I understood the race into the night. The tugging, my kneeling, my tears had not been for Katie alone, but also for a woman who was in trouble—a stranger on the other side of the planet whom God cared about deeply. She might as well have been me a thousand years ago when I'd been in trouble and needing help. How many people had God stirred to pray for me, not once, but many times over?

I bowed my head once again and was able to pray with clarity. I asked God to deliver the woman from bondage and to protect the team, "in Jesus' name."

My spirit reeled at God's pursuit of His lost sheep. The phone call was the prayer the Spirit brings, and confirmation of what great lengths God goes to save one soul. Mysteriously He uses others to accomplish His work. He could do it on His own, but instead He composes a song comprised of thousands of tiny voices to bring forth His voice, His message of salvation and hope.

Katie's request for others to join her in prayer brought a scripture verse to mind. The disciples could not cast out a demon, and they questioned Jesus. Jesus answered, *"This kind can only come out by prayer"* (Mark 9:29).

My Grandmother had often recited another verse as she prayed:

Again I say to you, if two of you agree on earth about anything they ask, it will be done for them by my Father in heaven. For where two or three are gathered in my name, there am I among them.

—Matthew 18:19–20, ESV

Still sitting in a state of awe and wonder, I returned the phone to its cradle. With the faint sound of white noise still crackling in my ears, I couldn't help but think of how we were so intimately connected. Katie and the stranger on the other side of the planet, and God, and me ...

Eventually Katie returned home, moved out, and moved on. We couldn't keep her to ourselves, but were privileged to see how the love of our heavenly Father keeps us together.

Katie is a gift from God, my running mate. She was my Good Samaritan who came along and nourished my soul. Through prayer and her example, I was able to reopen my home to many more, even in the face of further trials. Not all of the prayers we've prayed together have been answered; however, many are being answered now, long after our requests were made.

I have learned to trust God at a deeper level, even when life doesn't make sense. More importantly I have learned that my life is not my own. Everything belongs to Him.

Jesus, my Faith Keeper was whispering and weaving His family together, and revealing His power through the Spirit to help us finish the journey together.

Chapter Ten
Life is Short

All That is Grass

Seems like we're damned if we do, if we don't;
First we give birth, then we watch them leave home.
Wish I could tell you my heart's still in place,
But it broke the day you learned to say your first words.

Yesterday's fresh, but your body's a ghost.
Where did the promise of tomorrow go?
Wish I could tell you my heart beats the same,
But I laid it cold by your tombstone for flowers.

Oh, don't you feel sorry for me, funny
Cause lately I see honey,
That all that is grass fades away;
And don't you be worried about somethin'
We can't figure out; nothin' else matters,
But hearin' your name—whispered.

> Nobody cares what you carry inside;
> Bet you can tell by the look in my eyes,
> I've spent a life with my heart on my sleeve;
> Think I'd know by now that I can't breathe for others
> (But I can sure bleed).
>
> But don't you feel sorry for me, funny,
> Cause lately I see, honey,
> That all that is grass fades away;
> And don't you be worried about somethin'
> We can't figure out, nothin' else matters,
> But seeing your face—raptured.

"All That is Grass" from *My Heart's Lament* ©2010/Cindy Palin

Life is short. Yesterday I was a child aching to be a teenager. Hours ago I was a teen longing to be finished high school. Moments ago I watched my children leave the nest, and stood beside a hospital bed and said goodbye to a parent. As time evaporates, my Jesus and His faithfulness become clearer.

So much has happened since the stirring, reawakening, and surrendering. I look back down life's road and see a consistent pattern of Jesus, my Faith Keeper, pursuing and teaching, and drawing me into relationship with Him.

Once I made the decision to surrender to Jesus' plan for my life, my faith journey became less of a roller coaster ride and more like a dance. He gently leads me forward a few steps every day. There are times I step on His toes, moments when I forget to let Him lead. The music changes, but He's always there with His arms open towards me. But I must surrender in order to continue dancing.

His way, His song, and His dance are the best, where compromise and counterfeit cannot penetrate His gifts of peace and freedom. His boundaries and commandments are life and joy to my soul. Surrender is embracing His will completely with no tainted additions, no exceptions to His rule, no attempts to craft a rendition of my own design.

I have no shame of the scars I bear, because I am forgiven. They serve to help me remember just enough of who I was, to see how much He's changing me. I trudged the wider path with a ball and chain of condemnation. Now my step is light and unshackled on the road less travelled. His beautiful life- giving boundaries protect me from ever having to carry that extra weight again (Psalm 103:12).

I continue to learn so much about the way Jesus loves—through His Word, through marriage, through our children, and through the family of God we meet with regularly.

He is no stranger to the risk required to love and to suffer loss. I've felt Him hold me together when we've struggled with illness and watched our children leave the nest, and when we've said goodbye to our parents and friends, and I am always reminded that we are but grass.

For He knows how we are formed,
he remembers that we are dust.

> *The life of mortals is like grass,*
> *they flourish like a flower of the field;*
> *the wind blows over it and it is gone,*
> *and its place remembers it no more.*
>
> —Psalm 103:14–16

Especially during life's heart breaking moments, His resurrection plan has been powerfully beating in my heart, giving me the ability to let go of earthy things and prepare for Heaven. Even apprehension about growing old is gently met with His love, and sweetened with the gift of wisdom, continued purpose, maturity, and grandchildren.

I look around me and observe with compassion those who have not responded to His call. I mourn deeply over those who have heard the truth and made their promises, but have now traded the truth in for something else (Romans 1:25).

Is faith a word that conjures up some kind of religious checklist in your mind? Have you ever been introduced to Jesus, the person? Is the truth of a loving God too hard to grasp amidst world suffering? Does faith wear the face of blame, because someone's hurt you? Has your faith become a self-made formula much like I was trying to create once upon a time, where elements of truth and selfishness try to share the same bed? Can you see the difference between religion and relationship, and the importance of serving together? Are you willing to fall in love with Jesus, to surrender all and trust that He knows what your heart truly desires (Psalm 37:3–5)?

I hope you see the Faith Keeper reflected in these pages, and hear His voice in His words (scripture). Still your weary soul long enough to hear Him whisper. Be weak enough to need Him, and determined enough to seek Him with your whole heart, mind, and soul (Deuteronomy 4:26–30). You will not be disappointed. I pray you will hear your name whispered, and He will see your face raptured (1 Thessalonians 4:17). Take that leap of faith and let Him teach you how to live it out. Make that extra mile decision and finish the race: "*I have fought the good fight, I have finished the race, I have kept the faith*" (2 Timothy 4:7).

Life is a road marked with joy and suffering. Both are necessary to bring us closer to our Creator, Saviour, and friend. And long down the road when our hearts break, we'll finally know the Keeper of Faith. "*The one who calls you is faithful, and he will do it*" (1 Thessalonians 5:24).

Epilogue

My faith journey continues. The treadmill is always on the horizon, beckoning for me to jump back on. Old habits continually threaten to creep back in. I am constantly aware of my selfish introversion, and creative excuses, and relieved to know Jesus romances me still.

I am more of a team player than I've ever been. Without Christ I never would have been able to trust or risk loving anyone, and I continually ask Him to keep me surrendered.

Another lesson emphasized in *Experiencing God* by Henry T. Blackby is to watch for where God is at work at present, and join Him there, rather than drum up something of our own making and expect God to fit into our plans. Witnessing the difference found me on my knees praying another specific prayer: "Dear Jesus, bring your will to my door. I don't want to miss your will."

And that, my friend, is where the next story begins.

Resources

There are many more people I want to thank than those mentioned in this book, some of whom were there beside me or with me in prayer during these events. I trust there will be other opportunities to write about how their faith example has spurred me onward.

Shannon Ethridge Ministries
www.shannonethridge.com

Blackaby Ministries International
www.blackaby.net

Brian Daniel Nallathamby
Olds, Alberta
President - MEDIC Canada
www.mediccanada.org

Seed of Hope
www.theseedofhope.org

Heather Liebenberg
Amanzimtoti, Kwazulu-Natal, SA
Seed of Hope Community Development - Seed of Hope

Carl Waldron
Amanzimtoti, Kwazulu-Natal, SA
CEO - Seed of Hope

Michelle Waldron
Registered Nurse and Community
Health Team Leader at Seed of Hope - Seed of Hope

Canadian Charitable partner:
Hope Shares Canada
www.hopeshares.ca

United States partnership:
Rescue International
www.rescu.org

Katie Housek Peters
Abbotsford, BC. Canada
Mongolian mission trips: www.mennonitebrethren.ca

Tracey Mah-Gilles (@tmgfitness) Twitter
Calgary, AB. Canada
TMG Fitness/HITT Fitness Center

About the Author

Cindy and her husband, Lloyd Palin, are members of the First Baptist Church in Olds, Alberta, Canada. Cindy is currently working on her Bachelor of Christian Studies at Briercrest College and Seminary. She is a member of the Word Guild (www.thewordguild.com) and the Society of Composers, Authors, and Music Publishers of Canada (SOCAN). Cindy spends most of her time writing music, working with families in her community, and leading worship. She is a recording artist with five albums to her credit, which are available for purchase on iTunes. She and her husband own My Hometown

Framing, and Cindy can be found framing art weekday afternoons in their shop.

>She can be contacted through her website:
>www.newcindypalin.com